Pat
Asselin

M·A·R·I·L·Y·N

among friends

M·A·R·I·L·Y·N

among friends

SAM SHAW AND NORMAN ROSTEN

HENRY HOLT AND COMPANY / NEW YORK

First published in the United States in 1988 by
Henry Holt and Company, Inc., 115 West 18th Street,
New York, New York 10011.

Library of Congress Catalog Card Number: 88-80239.

ISBN 0-8050-0843-8

First American Edition

Designed by Roy Williams and Laurence Bradbury
Printed in Spain by Printer industria gráfica s.a., Barcelona
10 9 8 7 6 5 4 3 2 1
ISBN 0-8050-0843-8

The photographer Sam Shaw introduced Norman Rosten to Marilyn Monroe in 1955. Their relationship grew: Marilyn's analyst, Dr Ralph Greenson, described Rosten as one of her 'closest friends'. She married another of his friends, Arthur Miller, and from then on saw a great deal of Norman and his wife Hedda. And when she wasn't seeing them, she would phone – at all times of the day and night. Something in the gentle, humorous poet appealed to Marilyn and inspired her trust.

For Rosten, Marilyn was different things at different times: an attractive and vibrant woman, full of fun and energy; an innocent child with an appealing *naiveté*; and, on occasion, a dear friend, badly in need of help.

Photographer Sam Shaw met Monroe on the set of *Viva Zapata* when she was an out-of-work contract player. Shaw was to take many famous photographs of Marilyn, including the skirt-blowing shots for *The Seven-Year Itch*. But he too became her friend and over many years took the kind of photographs that only friends can.

200 of Shaw's intimate photographs, most of them previously unpublished, appear in this book. They reveal many facets of the Marilyn only her true friends knew: the sex goddess ravishing the camera on the beach at Amagansett; the wife shopping with husband Arthur Miller; the woman who longed for children relaxing with Rosten's young daughter Patricia; or the ethereal, virginal nymph dancing innocently among trees.

As her closest friends, both the author and photographer are uniquely placed to reveal the real Marilyn. *Marilyn among Friends* conveys its subject with greater authority, candour and, above all, affection than any previous book.

DEDICATION

To the actress
who strives or dreams
whether at liberty or stardom
taking on her own life and the lives of others
offering magic, pretending miracles

ACKNOWLEDGMENTS

Sam and Marc Weinstein, Color Group Photographic Laboratories

Larry Shaw, Susan Levy, Evelyne Scott-Hansen, Edith Marcus,
Mary Elizabeth Edelman, Mary Leatherbee, Tom Prideaux, Meghan O'Hearn

For permission to reproduce the lines from e.e. cummings' 'Puella Mea'
on p103, Grafton Books, a division of the Collins Publishing Group

CONTENTS

INTRODUCTION

THINGS TO BE SAID

Marilyn died in 1962; she was thirty-six. Each succeeding generation is drawn to the life and art of this remarkable woman. In half a dozen of her best films, from early walk-ons and one-liners to the emergence of a true comedienne, she left her imprint on cinema history. We keep returning to her life, and the suicide. Grade B melodrama? Greek tragedy? Or American tragedy? Or simply a life not fully realized, the fate of even the noblest strivers?

What more is there to know than the facts already so well known? The illegitimate child, the foster homes, the lure of Hollywood – moth and flame – and the passage of Norma Jean Baker to Marilyn Monroe. Stardom, world fame, marriages and divorce, the body broken, the dissolution of the spirit, and death. Today, we have a resurrection through memory; we have the victory of the pure in heart, the beautiful, and the lost. We take her seriously as an artist and person, a liberated woman before it became fashionable, who won an honored place and lost her life.

We shall leave behind the gossipmongers, journalists and charlatans; the self-proclaimed lovers out of the showbiz swamp; the writers knowingly dispensing fraud; the ex-cooks or ex-maids who sold their secrets (very few); all those who pretended to admire but mocked her decent ambitions; men who would not forgive her turndowns; hungry theorists who found her choice of dying too ordinary or not lucrative enough for the market and speculated on murder, CIA intrigue and Kennedy fantasies; the repeaters of slander and lies from the sexual gutters – her life interpreted, analyzed, pulled apart, pulled together – sensationalizing what were merely human failings. Why the mean-spirited review of her life, long after it was over? She had her share of lovers; she engaged in sex and apparently enjoyed it; she may have slept with one or more of the Kennedys: who's around to confirm or deny? Where and when and ho-hum. We leave that kind of history to the scavengers of the graves of the dead.

Our photographs and words present a woman of obscure beginnings who studied and struggled against great odds to create a life of dignity and respect. She confronted a world of caste and prejudice; she broke into the clear for herself and others.

We who offer this testament liked her, even loved her. We suffered her faults and follies, her tantrums and weaknesses, her difficult days on and off the set, along with her enchanting comic talent. Certain actors and studio executives scorned and vilified her. She had the last hurrah, hers was the joy of being alive and loving her work: the life recalled and held out to us in these sweet, haunting reminders.

1

AT THE
MAKE-UP TABLE

She returns to us as the camera's gift, the treasure of remembrance. She returns in echoes of dark and light, in a truth only the image can yield, the shutter's eye which sees and tells.

The image of Marilyn haunts and flowers from generation to generation. There are not many of her kind. She was born to film, that illusion transforming life into the reality of art.

At the make-up table, out of light and dark, with her brushes and colors, she prepares to enter that other dimension, born of herself. As actress. As magician. As woman. The mystery is hidden in light and shadow, revealed and hidden again, the endless search for identity that is the actor's obsession. Can one become lost in that search, and finally lost to life itself? Was this Marilyn's fate, the inability to hold on to the day-to-day connections with real people and events?

The make-up table. The craft of illusion. The entrance into the labyrinth from which some never return.

The camera loved Marilyn, and she loved the camera, more than her lovers, and husbands, and even her fans.

Half-dressed, she applies her make-up by the light of a tiny lamp with only a 20- or 40-watt bulb. The amber glow forces her to accent eyebrows, lashes, eye shadow, lipstick. The camera and director are waiting outside her dressing room, and farther out in time and space, in movie houses throughout America and the world, her audience waits.

Sam recalls: 'I would say to her, "Marilyn, when I'm shooting you, I don't want to shoot a pretty girl. I want to shoot an actress at work. I want to show how a picture is made — with sweat, struggle, disarrayed hair — to show the evolution of the professional beauty, the professional actress. I want to shoot you at work, at play, as you are. Be free, no phoney poses. Remember the camera loves you and if you wear all that make-up I feel I'm shooting Max Factor, Revlon or Estée Lauder, and not you."'

She says, 'I have a bulbous nose.' And she'd spend three hours before call time on her make-up; her make-up man Whitey Snyder would do the rest. Marilyn was fastidious about certain real or imagined 'defects'. Her nose for one. And her breasts: she did exercises to strengthen them 'to defy gravity', she said.

She had leg worries. She told Sam she had rickets as a child which affected her leg muscles; she was very careful about lighting when she posed. She knew how to control anything bad the camera might reveal; they understood each other very well.

Sam repeats, 'Marilyn, that make-up is a little overdone.'

She replies, 'Sam, you don't understand the public. This make-up is for my fans, those people waiting inside the movie houses, or outside in the street waiting in the crowd at an opening. They are the people the studios won't let close to the theatre unless they pay to get in. When I arrive there I'll turn and wave to them and they'll see me and won't be disappointed. My fans want me to be glamorous. I won't let them down.'

The camera's gift

She'd do things with the shadows on her nose . . .

*. . . she knew how to control anything bad the
camera might reveal*

AUTHOR CONFERENCE

OK, Sam. She liked to call you Sam Spade. Why the alias?

Her sense of fun. Why did Marilyn call you Claude, for Claude Rains?

Because I was, maybe still am, suave, warm, not bad looking, which was what the real Claude was.

What did she call Eli Wallach, do you know?

Yes, it was Tea House. Eli, you remember, was in *The Tea House of the August Moon* on Broadway. Marilyn loved the title and tagged him with it. I like it. One thing, she referred to me, you and Eli as the three men she most could trust. We were her brothers – she used that word.

So that's how we wind up, eh? As brothers. Okay. Lovers can be a problem. And it's good to have someone's trust.

That's because we were all family men, Sam. Marilyn, who never had a family, or enjoyed family warmth, she got it from us, our wives, and kids.

You think they'd believe us out there?

That's their problem.

Norman, what about her other nicknames?

Well, Arturo was an affectionate tag for Arthur. Poppycock for the dog. She had some cute names for herself, too. She once signed a short note with: 'Noodle, Sam, Max, Clump, Sugar, Finny, Pussy and all the rest.' A game of identity, the playful imp. That was an appealing part of her character. She had a great sense of humor. I think much of her humor comes from early adversity, you know, either it kills you or you can laugh about it. She had a sweet laugh.

This is my favorite

She had this photo in her scrapbook. Written in
multicolored crayon beside it were the words
'This is my favorite'

2

EARLY DAYS

Marilyn was born 'in a trunk' – a backstage baby. Her mother was a wardrobe mistress; years later she said her mother was a film editor. Marilyn wandered in and out of the studios. When she was a kid, it was a closed shop. She was one of them, among friends. The wardrobe departments regarded her as one of their own kind.

When Sam Shaw first met Marilyn, in 1951 or '52, she was unknown. Sam recalls: 'She was a contract player at 20th Century-Fox, on the layoff period until they picked up her contract, two months or so. A darling girl, a darling young woman. She used to drive me to location when I was covering *Viva Zapata*. Some of the photographs I made of Marilyn when she wasn't known, the post office wouldn't let the magazine they were in (*Argosy*) through the mail. I had given her one of my sports shirts which she wore open, shirt tails tied at the waist, her cleavage just barely showing. She was wearing a pair of jeans with a frayed fly. I can't get these photographs now: Edward Steichen asked for them and kept them.

'Marilyn once told me she never expected to be a star. She tought she would go from one studio to another, make a rotation of all the studios. She thought she would always be a pretty girl, a starlet. But when Johnny Hyde, her agent and an early lover, discovered her, her world expanded. She studied at UCLA at night, making friends among writers and musicians. At that time, she was like all the young women today, she made her own fashions, ahead of her time. She was among the first to wear jeans. She would get a new pair of jeans from an Army-Navy outlet store,

'She was among the first to wear jeans'

Wardrobe mistress Ruth and Marilyn –
discussing coffin decor?

go to Santa Monica beach, go into the sea, drenching the jeans till they clung to her body, then stay in the sun. The jeans dried to her form like a leotard. She said panties would interrupt the flow of the line.

'To me, she wasn't a calendar girl, although Tom Kelly's nude shot was the greatest calendar-type photo. She was a contemporary Aphrodite who could transform herself into a counter girl, a waitress, a beach playmate. She was every teenager we see today in jeans. She could never pour herself into a Cardin, Courrèges or Chanel.'

In those days, when layoff time came up, the studios cut off all monies. As a young starlet, Marilyn couldn't afford changes of clothes to go out on a date or to a dance, but that was never a problem. On call or off salary, the wardrobe department was there to help. Marilyn had the pick of the 20th Century-Fox wardrobe department! True, the gowns were dated and mostly ill-fitting at the bosom. That never bothered her, it amused her. The grips – a very closed sect – also regarded her as one of their own. She often asked them what she could do to add some color to her character;

they would help her improvise a piece of business such as a near-sighted dame who would always bump into furniture when she didn't wear glasses. These men behind the camera had seen every scene-stealing stunt since the silent screen days and knew how to help a buddy of the trade. During make-up time they'd clown and joke; one of their running gags was about the shape she'd use for her coffin and the style of the sheer black négligé she'd be draped in. Whitey was pledged to do the make-up and Ruth (wardrobe) the coffin layout.

*Whitey Snyder puts the finishing touches to
Marilyn's make-up*

3

THE PRESS, OR WHY THEY LOVED HER

In Hollywood, in the late forties, even before she worked for 20th Century-Fox as a starlet, Marilyn and the press got on famously together. She was good copy, and made good cheesecake photos for the girlie mags. She used to drive columnist Sidney Skolsky around to the studios (Sidney didn't drive); he was the first to write stories about her. When she came to New York she met Leonard Lyons who took up where Skolsky left off. They were moving her along, she impressed them. Lyons set up luncheons for her with the then reigning VIPs such as Pulitzer Prize-winning playwright Sidney Kingsley, David Wayne and Richard Adler who recommended her for his musical *The Pajama Game* (she didn't take the part, she felt she wasn't ready). Mary Leatherbee, *Life* movie editor, and Tom Prideaux, *Life* entertainment editor, met her. They were first to print a cover story. *Life* also printed her last interview, by Richard Merriman, taped several days before her death. Marilyn considered it the best ever.

Photographers discovered her – Phillippe Halsman, Richard Avedon, Milton Greene, Bert Stern, Jimmy Kavallines of the *Herald Tribune* – and Marilyn was well on her way. Sam was one of her early discoverers. He introduced her to the *Life* magazine editors and became a faithful friend.

The press followed her antics, delighted in her one-liners, gave her the publicity breaks she needed. Everything seemed to work to her advantage. When the famous nude calendar photo made its appearance in 1949 – an explosive event in that conformist era – the

Studio went into shock. Marilyn defused the issue with her explanation: the human body was nothing to be ashamed of and she had to pay her rent. Who dared to deny the body or the rent? The public loved this stuff.

Cover girl

Her ambition was to appear in Vogue *and* Harper's Bazaar. *Who else but famous photographer Richard Avedon?*

Look at me

The style at that time was tall, thin and elegant –
Suzy Parker, Dorian Leigh and Anne St Marie.
Marilyn had her own style

She was the darling of columnists such as Walter Winchell and personal friend Earl Wilson, and others. She had the wit and camaraderie to spar with reporters and give them their daily bread: 'Nothing but the radio,' she replied when asked what she had on. She seemed to have the talent and humor to give on-the-spot answers to questions, making it all appear reasonable.

Q: 'What do you wear when you go to bed, Marilyn?'

A: 'Chanel Number Five. Now and then I switch to Arpège.'

Q: 'Do you have any love interest now?'

A: 'No, no serious interests. But I'm always interested.'

Her witticisms were often steeped in a technical knowledge of the business. During the shooting of a scene at a bar in *Bus Stop*, she asked director Josh Logan for a close-up of her. He agreed it was a good moment, but asked, 'How could I shoot a close-up in Cinemascope? [a new method in film photography] I would have to crop off the top of your head.' To which Marilyn replied, 'That's all right. In the previous set-up you established that I have a top to my head.' Even Logan had to join in the laughter.

Set 'em up!

The press made her famous: cynical editors were charmed by this young woman in her late twenties who could hold her own with the pros in the number one drinking-hole in America, the 21 Club

Marilyn giving Broadway columnist Earl Wilson another of her witty one-liners

Bob Kriendler showing Marilyn rare trophies at the 21 Club

Overleaf:
At Billy Reed's: Marilyn's first outing in New York City after her 'independence' from Hollywood, hosted by Leonard Lyons (second from right). The others, reading from left to right: David Wayne, Marilyn herself, Milton Greene, Billy Reed and Sidney Skolsky

*Marilyn's first exploration of New York's theatre,
visiting Broadway stars backstage. Here she visits
the late Carole Hainey*

Billy Wilder was impressed with her comic talent. He saw her as akin to the Mae West character, and suggested that by creating her unique comedy style she could work in films until she was eighty.

Marilyn had the rare quality of attracting the fascination if not the company of writers and artists: Dylan Thomas, Jackson Pollock, Mark Rothko, Carl Sandburg, Andy Warhol, de Kooning, Tom Wesselman, a host of Monroe watchers. Her era coincided with the emergence of Pop Art: she became their icon, especially in New York.

Director Billy Wilder asked Marilyn to do a 'send-up' of Mae West, satirising Miss West's imitation of gay men. Marilyn, supremely feminine, lacked the element of hostility and ridicule toward men that would be essential in such impersonations. She flunked the test

ON THE TELEPHONE

Sam Spade? Why don't you and Anne meet me for
cocktails at five o'clock in Bungalow Ten at the Beverly
Hills Hotel?

I'm doing a wonderful scene at the Studio with Eli. What
an actor. Have you got a minute? Is Claude around? Keep
an eye on him, he loves you but you know these poets . . .

Hello. Is anybody up? I thought we could meet for coffee
somewhere.
Marilyn, it's 2:30 *AM*
Where's Hedda?
She's asleep. And I will be as soon as I hang up on you,
darlin', much as I hate to do it . . .

Hey, Marlon . . . never mind what am I doin', what are
you doin'? or not doin'? You liked that scene? Lee thought
I was making progress, so maybe I am . . .

C'mon, Josh . . . what've you got against him? He doesn't
look warm enough in that scene? He'll look hot if I can get
closer maybe, I mean, rub-a-dub-dub . . .

No, I can't, I have my head doctor late afternoon, or he
has *my* head, or something. Call me later, alligator!

4

PRIVATE
STAR WARS 1952

Joe DiMaggio did not have a movie smile but a decency showed in his face. That might have attracted Marilyn; she'd had enough of the brash Hollywood type. He was a famous baseball player, a great American athlete, serious, dedicated, well-mannered, light years away from the showbiz sleaze. He may have been over his head with Marilyn, yet he met and pursued – or, as some would have it, was pursued by – and married another 'player' and the world wished them well. They were acclaimed America's Hero and Heroine!

For Marilyn it was a period of preparation for one of her biggest hits, a turning point in her young career, *The Seven Year Itch*. Throughout their relationship, Joe was the star; she became the star after that movie and the divorce that followed. He remained a spectator in a setting where he was never fully at ease. A bittersweet romance at best. But DiMaggio was a gentleman, he never went public with his problems, he never gossiped. One can fairly imagine he suffered in silence.

In 1954, during the Korean War, Marilyn was invited to sing to the American troops. Joe was not very happy about it; he stayed in Tokyo while she went on to Korea. She arrived at the front by helicopter. She recorded it in her own words: 'It was cold and starting to snow. I was backstage in dungarees. Out front the show was on. I could hear music playing and a roar of voices to drown it out. An officer came backstage. "You'll have to go on ahead of schedule. I don't think we can hold them any longer. They're throwing rocks on the stage." The noise I'd been hearing was

my name being yelled by the soldiers. I changed quickly into my silk gown. It had a low neckline and no sleeves. I felt worried all of a sudden about my material, not the Gershwin song but the other I was going to sing – "Diamonds Are A Girl's Best Friend". It seemed like the wrong thing to say to soldiers in Korea, earning only soldier's pay. Then I remembered the dance I would do after the song. It was a cute dance. I knew they would like it.' She confided to columnist Sidney Skolsky upon her return home: 'I felt I belonged . . . I told Joe that for the first time I felt like a movie star.' What Joe had to say about her adventures, we'll never know.

The Seven Year Itch spelt doom for the Marilyn/Joe relationship, for it contained the scene later to be called 'the shot seen round the world' – the famous skirt-blowing episode with Marilyn standing over the sidewalk grating laughingly trying to keep her skirt down and not entirely succeeding, with co-star Tom Ewell looking on bemused and somewhat interested. The draught rising up through the grating was carefully generated by a wind-machine installed below, which also added the subway noise. The area was cordoned off, thousands showed up, well-behaved, enjoying every moment while Marilyn enjoyed it along with the crowd. It was basically a comic scene, but it shocked DiMaggio who was watching the filming that day. He stormed off the set in anger. He was newly married, he didn't like his wife in that situation, yet it was a commonplace Hollywood turn, showing America that their rising star had beautiful legs. Again,

Marilyn and DiMaggio

On the town in New York, playing the big leagues

*Johnny Graham (third from left), East Coast
production manager who set up the logistics of
the spectacular scene*

Rehearsing the shot

and not to be forgotten, Marilyn came through as the flower of innocence, sex as good clean fun. America would love it, her, the scene, woman, symbol – the whole package. By next morning it was front page in London, Paris, Rome, Berlin, Tokyo, the whole world. But Joe was clearly unhappy. This was the entertainment capital of the world, fantasyville, peeping-tom land, Hollywood, and you learned to play the game.

Joe's game was baseball.

Marilyn, in her own way, respected his world, and its meaning for him. After their divorce, Joe and Marilyn (on a date) joined Sam and his wife Anne at Manny Wolf's restaurant in New York, on 49th and Third Avenue, a famed steakhouse for sports lovers, basically a man's hangout. On this particular evening, Joe was the special attraction; soon a number of men and their teenage sons stopped by their table, asking for Joe's autograph

on slips of paper, or menu cards. He was the center of attention here. 'The interesting thing,' said Sam about that evening, 'Was Marilyn's attitude. She was proud of Joe, you could tell. She was beaming. She was not in the least bit hurt by watching Joe have his share of glory, you could see she had the highest respect for this man. She didn't know too much about baseball, but she knew he had millions of fans, even as she had. She knew what it must have meant to him, the pride of his art. She could understand that.'

And I could recall a scene in another famous restaurant, Chasen's in Beverly Hills, years after that separation, when my wife and I were joined by Marilyn and her escort William Inge. She had earlier starred in *Bus Stop*, based on Inge's hit play; my accidental meeting with Inge led to this impromptu dinner foursome. Bill Inge, solemn and friendly, was lamenting the decline of the authority of the

screen writer. 'I must have labored on *Bus Stop* for over a year, only to watch it being changed from day to day during the shooting. Then I realized the script is merely a skeleton for the director.' With a courteous ironic smile toward Marilyn, he added, 'And maybe for the actress who loves to add a line or two in her speech.'

Marilyn laughed. 'You writers are always complaining. Why can't we help our character with our own insights, you know, to help what's on the page?'

'Because, dear lady,' Bill replied gently, 'Actors aren't writers, and get paid only to act.'

'I'm hungry, let's order,' said my wife, with her pragmatic wisdom.

'And I don't want to talk shop,' I said, 'Not on this lovely evening in Paradise.'

Marilyn waved to someone across the large room. To our surprise, a man quietly approached our table and greeted her with a slight bow. It was Joe DiMaggio, the second of her three ex-husbands. He gave Inge a curious but not unfriendly stare, putting him instantly at ease. Inge, unhappy at the possibility of being romantically linked with Marilyn, soon relaxed. Joe remained standing as he reached over for Marilyn's hand and pressed it, then turned and acknowledged her introductions. We were all delighted to meet him. One could sense a warm feeling between these two star-crossed lovers. It was a far cry from their dating years, sitting in the Beverly Hills Hotel with Joe's PR buddy, Bernie Kamber, with Joe watching baseball on TV for hours, fol-

Hold the front page!

51st Street, Lexington Avenue, Borough of Manhattan, USA, where the shot seen around the world was taken – front page from New York to California, including London, Paris, Rome, Berlin, Tokyo . . .

The man who operated the wind-machine under the grating for the skirt-blowing shot

lowed by a stretch of westerns. Marilyn sat next to him all the time, not understanding one play from another, yet desiring his company. It seemed to me, observing them now, that they should have been the happily-ever-after couple among her three marriages. She and Joe had a similar street-smart air, a tough instinct for survival, that might have served them well in the years to come. But a longing in her stirred to the music of a different drummer, a music that led her to a more ambitious and dangerous love. Miller, like DiMaggio, was a quiet man, with deep inner drives, centered less on others than on himself. And Marilyn, looking for a safe haven, turned toward him and the perilous adventures of art.

But at that moment, with Joe standing by, asking her about her new film in preparation, he appeared a steadfast friend. His fist playfully against her jaw, he said, 'Best of luck, kid. You have what it takes.' Yet he knew, this athlete who set a record of consecutive base hits in a glorious career, that every string must run out.

5

'ACTOR'S TRUTH'

On a film set, a 'nude' actor, say under a bedsheet, generally wore underwear. Such precautions were taken in case the covering should accidentally be whisked off by a prop person. Horrors! Nudity in a town where nudity is unknown!

Or, in a bathtub, the actress (men are rarely seen in baths, usually in macho show-ers) might be required suddenly to change position or rise abruptly. Horrors again in a town where a soap-covered female nude is a sacrilege! Thus, even in a bubble-bath shot, a few emergency clothing items were worn.

But Marilyn insisted on being nude under the coverings. She wanted 'to be true to the situation and character.' She called it 'actor's truth'. This attitude was instinctive and not as a result of the Method or her tuition from the master teachers Michael Chekhov and Lee Strasberg. She was great on instinct. She asked, 'Would *you* take a bath, bubble or not, wearing panties and a bra?'

Nude in real life, nude beneath the suds! While Victor Moore, who played a plumber in *The Seven Year Itch*, looked on and seemed to enjoy it.

Don't peek!

Marilyn between takes (with cinematographer Milton Krasner in the background)

Acting coach Natasha Lytess takes Marilyn
through her lines

That's not fair!

Billy Wilder sneaks a kiss from a captive Marilyn

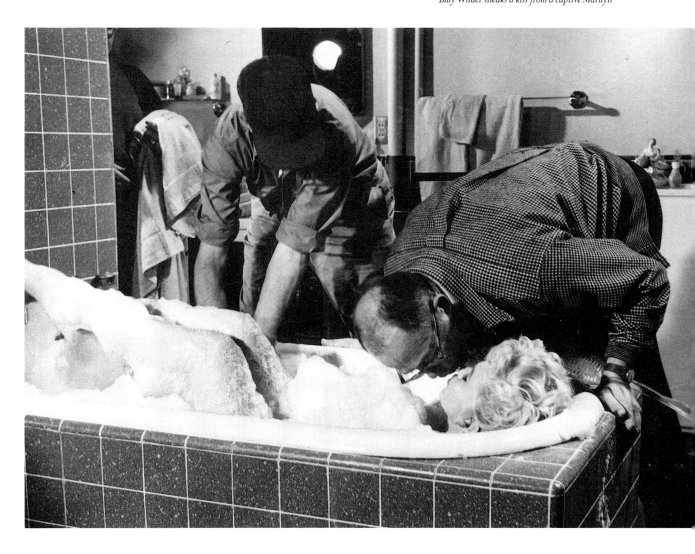

6

THE GIRL WITH NO NAME

Film writer George Axelrod said: 'I have seen at least twenty different actresses play the part of the Girl in my play *The Seven Year Itch*. I have seen the Girl as a blonde, a brunette, and a redhead. I've heard her say her lines with a British accent, in French, in Italian, in German. Many of the actresses have been wonderful in the part. A few have been a little less wonderful. But only one has ever come really close to playing the part exactly the way I imagined it when I first wrote it.

'Marilyn Monroe doesn't just play the Girl. She *is* the Girl. Marilyn once told me that playing the part had helped her to find out who she was. Which is a pretty nice thing for a writer to hear from an actress.

'I am revealing no breathtaking secret when I say that Marilyn has a reputation for not being the easiest actress in the world to work with. Her eagerness and ambition cause her to tense up. She has difficulty remembering lines. She has been known to drive directors stark, raving mad. However, an interesting thing happened during the shooting of *Itch*. My favorite scene in the picture comes close to the end. It is a kind of serious and extremely difficult scene in which the Girl explains to the hero (who, to all outward appearances, is the least dashing, least glamorous, least romantic man alive) why she finds him exciting and attractive and why his wife has every reason to be jealous.

'Because of its difficulty and the fact that it ends with a long speech from the Girl, it was generally assumed that the scene would need several days to get on film. Billy Wilder

Scenes on the set of The Seven Year Itch

patiently struggled through dozens of takes for every scene except this one. Three minutes later it was all over. Marilyn had done it, letter perfect and with an emotional impact that caused the entire soundstage to burst into applause at the end, on the first take. There was no need for a second.

'She told me later she was able to do the scene because she believed every word of what she was saying and because it seemed to her like the story of her own life. As it might be interesting to see what it is that Marilyn so firmly believed in, here's the end of the scene as it appears in the shooting script:

(SCENE 85. LIVINGROOM. DAY. TWO SHOT. RICHARD AND THE GIRL)

RICHARD

Let's face it – no pretty girl in her right mind wants *me*. She wants Gregory Peck . . .

THE GIRL

How do you know what a pretty girl wants? You think every pretty girl is a dope. You think that a girl goes to a party and there is some guy – a great big hunk in a fancy striped vest, strutting around like a tiger – giving you that 'I'm so handsome, you can't resist me' look – and from this she is supposed to fall flat on her face. Well, she doesn't fall flat on her face. But there's another guy in the room . . . way over in the corner . . . maybe he's kind of nervous and shy and perspiring a little . . . First you look past him, but then you sort of sense that he is gentle and kind and worried, that he'll be tender with you and nice and

sweet, and that's what's really exciting!

If I were your wife, I'd be jealous of you . . .
I'd be very, very jealous.

(She kisses him)

I think you're just elegant!

'I have been asked if there is any symbolic significance in the fact that the Girl has no name. The truth of the matter is that I could never think of a name for her that seemed exactly right, that really fit the girl I had in mind. I think if I were writing the play today, I might be tempted to call the Girl Marilyn.'

Commercial break

In the midst of meeting production schedules of
$10,000 a day, Billy Wilder stops for a reflective
moment before filming a satire on TV
commercials which holds up very well today

Phew!
Marilyn cooling off

Marilyn posing with a young man for a publicity still

Old fashioned Hollywood

Booms, lights, cameras, grips and gaffers up in
the grids, to capture a single moment in the life of
a film

Exterior . . . interior – New York in the East 60s

7

LIFE GOES TO A PARTY

From the legendary Grauman's Chinese Theatre in Hollywood where the young Marilyn had tried to fit her foot in the cement prints of the famous movie stars, it was more than a trip across town to Romanoff's in Beverly Hills where the slightly older, wiser, now glamorous Marilyn was given a party by director Billy Wilder and producer Charlie Feldman upon completion of *The Seven Year Itch*. It was *Life* magazine's weekly feature 'Life Goes To A Party' (issue of November 29th, 1954). A party for her, in her honor. The starlet had *arrived*!

This was Hollywood indoors; outdoors you'd get crisscrossing searchlights in the night sky, and people. The party was not open to the public. But we can say – and Sam Shaw, who was there as her escort and court photographer, can attest – that Marilyn was truly and warmly welcomed into the select circle following the success of *The Seven Year Itch*. She was the most likeable and dazzling star to move across the Hollywood heavens. She had arrived and she had paid her dues: hard work, low pay, the starlet routine of runaround and humiliation. But here she was on her special evening, pure, pristine, her scars hidden by the make-up of her trade, her spirit surmounting all, aglow with joy and innocence: the Marilyn who could combine sexual allure with the playfulness of a child as easily as one breathes. Whatever the formula, she had it; she came out of her corner smiling, gracious, low-cut, and they loved it.

The aristocracy of Hollywood turned out: men of power, studio heads who fought to retain the slavery of the contract player (those same men who would soon give battle to the rebel Marilyn, and lose); women of fashion as well as power; wives; stars of the primary and lesser galaxies – Darryl Zanuck, Jack Warner, Sam Goldwyn, Humphrey Bogart, Gary Cooper, Groucho Marx, Clifton Webb, George Burns, Lauren Bacall, Susan Hayward, Jean Howard, Clark Gable, Loretta Young, Roland Petit, Charles Vidor, Irving Lazar, Jean Negulesco, amongst others. They were all there. And more.

at the Life party

Marilyn, Clark, Sidney Skolsky and a cut-out of you know who . . .

Kay Gable, Marilyn and Clark

Far left:
Standing left: Humphrey Bogart and fascinated
unidentified waiter. Seated left to right: Henry
Hathaway, Gary Cooper, Kay Gable, Hjordis
Tersmeden (Mrs David Niven) and Darryl F.
Zanuck with his omnipresent cigar

Left: Billy Wilder and Evelyn Keyes

Below: Virginia Zanuck and Susan Hayward

When she met Clark Gable, Marilyn was as thrilled as any teenager. They were seated together at the same table, the King and the new princess. Her biggest thrill was asking for and getting Gable's autograph, 'the autograph I wanted since I was twelve years old,' she told him. Her costume was from 20th Century wardrobe – she didn't own a formal gown – and she had borrowed jewelry from Mrs Karger, the 'grande dame' of Hollywood society, so real they looked like real fakes.

Sam recalls: 'Tommy Ewell's and my hired tuxedos and patent leather shoes were from Western Costume: sewn pockets, no money, shoes too big. The maturing/aging beauties of Hollywood and the producers' wives wouldn't allow bright lights, only romantic candlelight glow. I had to borrow a flash camera from *Life* photographer Jack Birns. On the way to the party, neither Marilyn nor I had any money. Marilyn was high. It was the night of her life. No gas in the tank, she sweet-talked a gas station attendant for gas. In the doorway of the restaurant, a crowd of fans waited for her. She kept all the star-studded guests waiting inside while she posed for her fans who photographed her with their amateur cameras.'

Here's to you, my dear

Producer Charles Feldman toasting the new star
with Jean Howard and Clark Gable
eavesdropping

The autograph she wanted 'since I was twelve years old'

*Agent Ned Marin with Susan Hayward and
Clifton Webb*

French ballet stars Zizi Jean Maire and Roland Petit

Michael Rennie and Lauren Bacall

George Burns and a Swedish starlet, unidentified

Gary Cooper and Hjordis Tersmeden

Marilyn danced with the handsome and powerful: with Clark Gable and Humphrey Bogart, Darryl Zanuck and Clifton Webb; she danced with new friends and old. 'As I watched and photographed in the low-key light of Romanoff's, it struck me that she was a metaphor of Hollywood, a place of corny pictures, monstrous business people, monster movies, but also of serious film-makers, producers, writers, directors, actors, camera and crew men – all of them wanting to do their best. Marilyn kept wanting and trying to do her best.' This was an evening of triumph and high hopes for the future. As Marilyn would say later on, 'After all, I have come from way down.'

This was one of her 'up' moments. Definitely.

Star and producer

Cutting up with Clifton Webb

Clark and Marilyn: Dancing in the Dark

Lauren Bacall and agent extraordinaire Irving Swifty Lazar

Super-mogul Jack Warner doing the tango with a
Hollywood socialite

Audrey (Mrs Billy Wilder), who managed the Big
Party and its perilous risks of omissions and
commissions

The eternal Claudette Colbert

A rare rear view
Darryl F. Zanuck: the last tycoon, with Marilyn

Bogey, Marilyn and Clifton — three jolly good fellows

Action!
Billy Wilder, offstage, continues to direct Charles Vidor and mysterious companion

8

THE CORPORATE STAR WARS, OR THE SMART TOUGH BLONDE

Our heroine, that slip of a girl with a squeaky voice, was finding another voice. *The Seven Year Itch* was completed. Ambition and rebellion stirred within her. Now a superstar, with top billing, Marilyn did not intend to remain on a starlet salary. She looked ahead to more money, better stories, script approval, choice of director and other privileges unheard of for a young woman star. She had sensed her power; she was determined to test it. She was ready to enter the fray, to deal with lawyers, press agents, promotion people: in short, to deal. She entered the star wars.

The Corporate Voice listened and said 'No'. Big Daddy Spyros Skouras, president of 20th Century-Fox, could not sway the Board of Directors who looked upon actors as chattel. Nor could Darryl Zanuck. Both these giants were her 'friends' and yet were powerless to free her from the bonds of the contract player. Marilyn was caught in the battle by stockholders to take over 20th Century-Fox, an in-house struggle comparable to the takeover battles of today. She chose this time to break her contract with the studio, before *The Seven Year Itch* was released. It was a smart move, since they needed her to help make the movie a success; it was a gamble that paid off.

What the board didn't count on was the dumb blonde becoming a smart cookie and a tough one at that. Marilyn proved she was capable of fighting for her rights. New battles were shaping up. Plans were in the air. In her corner was Milton Greene, her new business partner, plus loyal agents, lawyers, and personal PR people. And Arthur Miller was in her

glass ball. She made the big move eastward – literally walked out – to exile, marriage and a future.

First came the stopover in England and a co-starring role in the film *The Prince and the Showgirl* with the world-renowned Sir Laurence Olivier. When she returned to Hollywood to fulfil her earlier contract commitments, she had a new weapon, an organization known as Marilyn Monroe Productions.

Two years later, Marilyn celebrated another hit, perhaps her most successful film, *Some Like It Hot*. Two years later in 1961, her last film *The Misfits*, written by Arthur Miller, directed by John Huston, and starring Marilyn, was released and her marriage to Miller ended. She had reached the heights, with barely two more years of her life remaining.

Big Daddy

Spyros Skouras (centre), President of 20th Century-Fox

*With Ed Sullivan, columnist and king of the TV
chat shows*

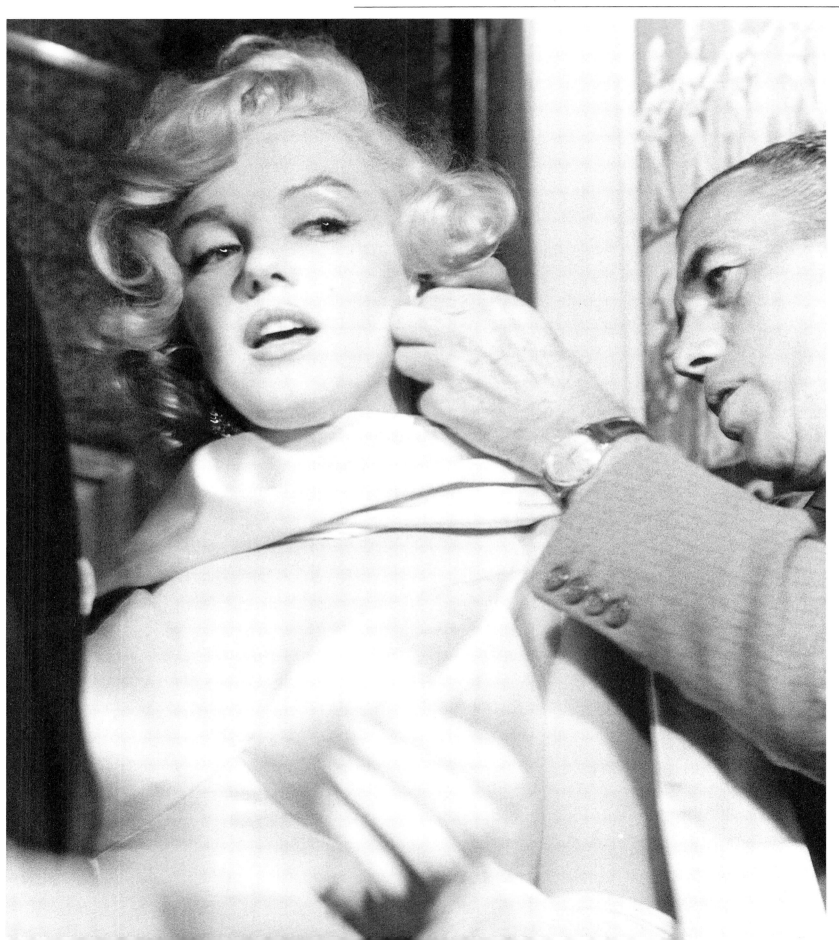

9

MARILYN VISITS SHANGRI-LA

Marilyn first visited Brooklyn on a rainy day in 1955 and it was because of the rain that we met. She had heard of this fabled land (as who has not?), it became in her mind a mythical place, and here it was at last, close by. And so was Arthur Miller, whom she had met several years earlier in Hollywood on a writing assignment. That may have been a further lure. At any rate, friend Sam gallantly became her guide for the day. They walked over the great Brooklyn Bridge, that stone and steel-suspended miracle, colossus anchored in tides, still surprising the landscape after a century.

They wandered through the streets shunting off from the bridge when fate intervened, as it often does in Brooklyn. It began to rain. From light to heavy. The phone rang, it was Sam. He said in his lively voice, 'If this is you, old buddy, and you still live in the same place, I need a port in a storm. Can you spare some coffee and shelter? I'm with a model who is drenched. We need a roof and a place to dry out.'

'Well, come over, both of you,' I replied. They did, half an hour later, the rain still heavy outside. From a second story curve in a mid-nineteenth century brownstone walk-up, I looked down as Sam and his model friend wearily mounted the stairs. I had not seen Sam for several years, he seemed agile and hearty and smiling as he came into closer view. Behind him was the model he introduced hurriedly as 'Marion' (or so I thought), both passing me as they entered the open doorway of the apartment. She whispered 'Thank you', holding an ankle-length camel-hair coat closely around her. (It was given to her by Johnny Hyde.)

The model was young and somewhat dampened by the rain, her light-colored hair straggly and uncombed. Her shoes and stockings were wet. She removed her coat and sat down quietly on the couch, her eyes taking in the furniture, the paintings on the wall, the bookcases. She was easily comfortable, like any stray cat finding a warm lucky pillow.

My wife Hedda enters, greeting Sam and our lady visitor with equal warmth, noting her wet shoes and offering a substitute pair of slippers. The model nods with a girlish smile. Hedda goes into the kitchen to set up coffee while Sam and I reminisce about my brief Hollywood experience years back and his own long labors in the showbiz vineyards. I tell him, 'You've had the opportunity all these years, decades, photographing the most beautiful screen personalities in the world, most of them women. You're lucky.'

Marion – I did not recognise her as anyone else – meanwhile had moved to the bookcase and picked out by chance a slim book. She examined it, leafing through several pages: a small volume of poems, entitled *Songs For Patricia*. She read silently, then turned to me.

'Who's Patricia?'

I reply, 'My daughter.'

'They're lovely poems, I'll have to get this book.'

I tell her, 'Take it with you. Consider it a little gift.'

She clutches the book to her body; her

Sam and Marilyn backstage

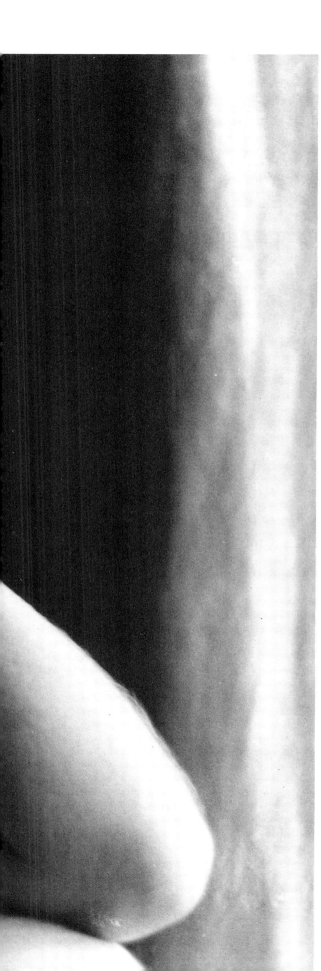

manner is shy, modest, and at this moment extremely interested.

'Oh, thank you.'

My wife has brought in hot coffee. She invites the model into the bedroom for a quick change of stockings and slippers. Then, more relaxed, we sit and enjoy the coffee.

Hedda asks her, 'Are you a New Yorker? Sam didn't say.'

'No. I'm from California, staying for a while. I'm studying at the Actor's Studio. I'm sort of an actress.' Her feet are drawn up under her; if she were a cat she'd purr.

'That sounds very exciting. Have you been in any plays?'

'Not really. Not yet. I've done some scenes. But I've done a couple of movies.'

'Any I should know, or have I missed them? What is your movie name?'

'Marilyn Monroe.'

My wife and I stare at her, not embarrassed but surprised. She smiles, then offers a little laugh.

Sam, silent until now, joins her laugh. 'Didn't I tell you? Or did I forget?'

'You introduced her as Marion.'

'Did I?' he responds slyly. 'One of my jokes. It's the Girl, genuine, also incognito. She's a friend of my camera. I hope she'll be your friend.'

Marilyn said later that we accepted her for herself, and she never forgot it.

Tea and vodka (2 to 1) along with smalltalk

10

THE ACTOR'S STUDIO: LOVE AND WORK

The Actor's Studio in New York was a crucial experience for Marilyn. It was there, in the mid-Fifties, that she attended classes and had her first contact with real theatre. It was there she met – either on her own or with introductions by Elia Kazan, Arthur Miller, and others – a group of young, hard-working and exciting actors who saw theatre as a mission, a training ground. Elia Kazan was a friend in Hollywood who had helped her in the early struggling years, and who introduced her to Arthur Miller. Miller said that he met the actress in 1950 when he visited the set of *As Young As You Feel*. As he recalls it, 'There was this girl crying in the corner, beautifully dressed, waiting to go on. She was so striking and so terribly sad. The combination struck me. I didn't know her at the time – along with ninety-eight per cent of America.'

The Studio (as it was called) nurtured those who would one day honor the profession: Marlon Brando, Eli Wallach, Maureen Stapleton, Kim Stanley, Montgomery Clift, Paul Newman, Julie Harris, Frank Silvera, Geraldine Page, Ben Gazzara, Ellen Burstyn, Eva Marie Saint, William Greaves, Elia Kazan, Joanne Woodward. The list is a long one, with many dozens of names.

The Studio was a place for actors, or acting students, to meet, discuss scripts, work on scenes, improvise, and generally become immersed in the origins and processes of theatrical expression. The head of the Studio was the renowned Lee Strasberg, teacher, critic, guru to some, tyrant to others, father figure or confidant to those who needed one

or both. In these roles he guided and often inspired a generation of actors; he introduced the work and theory of Stanislavski and taught its application to his own 'method' as teacher. For a migratory and lonely Marilyn, this was a new and exciting time, a way to break the Hollywood stalemate. The city beckoned with opportunities. She had had private classes with Michael Chekhov in Hollywood; he had been associated with the Moscow Art Theatre and was considered by many to be the greatest teacher of acting. Theatre people such as Josh Logan and Anthony Quinn studied with him. Marilyn told Sam that they did scenes from *King Lear*, with Chekhov as Lear, while she played Cordelia.

While Chekhov was helpful and instructive, Marilyn yearned to dip a foot into deeper waters. New York was the place. And she knew that Arthur Miller lived there, no small lure. She also came for business reasons, to discuss the setting up of Marilyn Monroe Productions with Milton Greene. It was a visit that was to affect her future. The Studio meanwhile offered an identity as well as new friends. It supplemented the family friendships she developed with Sam Shaw, Eli Wallach, and myself. To which we can add the Strasberg family, with two teenage children. And add further the social life of the Studio, often spent out in the country – relaxation from the gruelling hours of study and discipline. Then there were special events like the Actor's Studio Benefit where Marilyn and Marlon (Brando) played ushers for the $500 ticket holders: that was a super event for her! They became friends and dated briefly.

When Cheryl Crawford, a founder of the Actor's Studio, met Marilyn, she sent her with a recommendation to the head man, Strasberg. Marilyn began as an observer, not yet qualified to become a Studio member, a status which was conferred only after a series of auditions. Meanwhile, she was called upon to engage in what Stanislavsky called, among his many precepts, 'living the part'. Stanislavsky was clearly the bedrock of the Studio. More than advocating an acting method, he opened a path to the unconscious, to those areas of insight which can prove invaluable to the actor. During this period, Strasberg's support fused with Marilyn's desire to master the art of acting, to take her talent in a more ambitious direction. The mind, the body, the past, memory – all these elements were to be harnessed with hard work and study. The Studio was a sanctuary and a testing place for her, until the day when, after months of study, *le maître* felt Marilyn was ready to do a scene for Studio members, an audience of her peers. She was near the age of thirty.

The scene was from O'Neill's *Anna Christie*, an early naturalistic play about a rundown sea captain and his daughter. While it offered Marilyn a great opportunity in a slow-burning dramatic role, it had many pitfalls for a neophyte actress. Coached by Strasberg, after months of probing the character, and with Arthur Miller's unofficial aid, she made her final preparations. The father-daughter elements of the play touched some emotional

Lee Strasberg, Master of the Method, guru, tyrant, however you took him

Actor's Studio

Time out from Broadway on Elia Kazan's Connecticut acres

Marlon

Athlete, actor, batting over 300

*Eli at bat, also Marilyn's favorite dancing
partner (PS — he was a better dancer)*

nerves in her own life. Like Anna, Marilyn had been exploited by a foster family, and been sexually assaulted at sixteen by a cousin; there was a crossing of life and art here.

Her performance was startling. The film actress was now 'on stage' in a historic début. Strasberg had high praise for his pupil's ability to transmit more on the stage than on the screen. Somehow – whether through instinct or desperation – Marilyn found the key to the character. Those who came to scoff remained to marvel. Kim Stanley, one of the sceptics, thought Marilyn's performance was 'just wonderful. She *was* wonderful. We were taught never to clap at the Actor's Studio – it was like we were in church – and it was the first time I'd ever heard applause there. Some of us went to her privately and apologized.' And actors rarely apologize – or praise.

Eli Wallach and Marilyn became friends while they were both attending the Actor's Studio. As with myself and Sam Shaw, she moved into the Wallach family orbit, enjoying the company of those two stellar actors, Eli Wallach and Anne Jackson, who starred singly or together in many productions on Broadway and with touring groups. Marilyn was often a baby-sitter for their children.

When she first came to New York in 1954, Eli invited her to see him in the starring role of the long-running hit play *The Teahouse of the August Moon*. He sensed that she had never attended a professional production of a play. She was overwhelmed, mesmerized by the production and its company of polished actors. Here was an art form where the direc-

tor didn't interrupt scenes with cries of 'Cut!' Marilyn came to her classes and exercises with awe, observing in silence, feeling out this new artistic home. It was to be merely an interlude, for several Hollywood commitments still awaited her. But she worked hard, she proved to herself that she was capable of this dream.

(Miller would later doubt her ability to act on the stage. Though appreciating her seriousness, he realized as a man of the theatre that she lacked the discipline and training to enter the world of continuous on-stage tension, without two or three or ten takes per scene. The stage was not a medium for close-ups, but for deeper, more sustained psychological exploration and awareness.)

During a class break, Eli and Marilyn were having lunch in a restaurant overlooking Broadway. Across the street, workmen were hoisting a huge sign into place showing Marilyn's famous skirt-blowing scene from *The Seven Year Itch*, which had opened to great fanfare in 1955. Marilyn observed it for a moment, then turned to Eli and said, 'That's all they're interested in.'

Her success in facing a live audience infused Marilyn with new confidence as she prepared a return to Hollywood for her next film, *Bus Stop*. And with it came audacious plans to break with the star system and take control of her destiny.

Marilyn and David Wayne

11

MARILYN AND JOE: BITTERSWEET BLUES

After the divorce, Marilyn and Joe were living in New York, they dated and were still friends. Joe was her escort to the Broadway premiere of *The Seven Year Itch*. Now the tables were turned and *he* was the romantic pursuer. But Marilyn only wanted his friendship. From then on, he was her dependable buddy in times of crisis.

This was Marilyn's great period: new friends in New York, getting caught up in the excitements and rhythms of the great city, going to the Actor's Studio as an observer and then as an active participant. Studying with Lee Strasberg, the dean of teachers, to be a better actress in the company of important actors and actresses of the theatre. She renewed her friendship with Arthur Miller. A whole new world opened up for her.

Marilyn was discovering herself.

Joe DiMaggio leaves New York. He goes to Paris and then to Rome. He has a desire to see where his mother and father came from. In Rome, he meets Roberto Rossellini, the director of *Open City*; Rossellini, the hero of another international romance – with Ingrid Bergman – for whom he gave up Anna Magnani, one of the greatest actresses of our time. Rome welcomes Joe with dignity and grace. Wherever he wanders the Italians, young and old, recognize their American baseball hero. He decides to go to Sicily where his parents were born and married . . . Isola delle Femmine. Island of women. (When the men went off to sea, fishing to make a spare living for the family, the island became a village of women in black.)

When Joe arrives (by bus), townspeople, kids and adults recognize him – obviously his pictures had been page one even in the smallest village in Italy – the *numero uno* athlete of America. Again he is greeted by young and old with a welcome smile and a nod of recognition. In Isola delle Femmine, Joe meets the DiMaggios, a cousin who was a lawyer and mayor of the town, other cousins – the village could have been named DiMaggio, there are so many of them. They remind him that they were originally settled by the Greeks of antiquity. Joe discovers that he is not only an Italian-American but that he has strong Grecian roots.

Just as Marilyn, far away from her home-town base of Los Angeles, is discovering herself in New York, Central Park and Brooklyn, Joe is discovering himself in Sicily where his mother and father came from and were married.

Joe had his family; Marilyn was yet to find hers.

*Whee —
its me
M.M.*

Free and hopeful

Joe D

In Rome on a lonely journey

When in Rome

With some American expatriates on the
glamorous Via Veneto

A SMALL PERSONAL WORLD

Marilyn, walking through Central Park with Sam, was explaining Strasberg's concept of 'sense memory' and its use to an actor, especially in improvisation. She said, 'I'm doing Anna Christie and I'm feeling rain, you get the idea?'

'Show me an improvisation,' Sam countered, 'Right now.'

Marilyn picked up a copy of the *New York Times* and walked over to a nearby park bench where a young couple were engrossed in conversation.

She sits beside them, apparently oblivious to them and their conversation. She unfolds a newspaper, creating a small personal world. They pay no attention to her and continue their dialogue. The young man is proposing marriage. Marilyn is totally absorbed in the paper.

When the 'exercise' was completed, Marilyn turned to them, explained her purpose and asked them for permission to use the photos. They agreed.

I'm concentrating

Improvisation in Central Park: 'Sense memory'

12

POPCORN
AND HUZZAH

Marilyn liked people and crowds – she was definitely not the recluse type – but some who accompanied her on public missions did not. I did not. She confided that crowds could be scary, yet she knew their power in her behalf: '. . . and I want to say that the people – if I am a star – the people made me a star. No studio, no person, but the people did.'

It is well to keep in mind that she came out of neighborhoods of working people (she worked in a factory during World War II), the kind she could trust, the kind who would later come to her movies just to see her smile, and walk, and turn with a flick of her hips that was naughty but nice. Few, if any, movie stars gained such mass reactions, not Ava Gardner, Elizabeth Taylor or even the great Garbo. Hers was the popcorn and huzzah crowd. Later though, with fame, she proved she could mingle easily with all levels of society, from the Queen of England (during the filming of *The Prince and the Showgirl* in London), personalities as varied as Dame Edith Sitwell and Isak Dinesen (Karen Blixen), and the American poet Carl Sandburg, to the doorman of her building, and the crowds, the anonymous ticket-buyers, all those from whom she derived her energy and confidence. She took to publicity with ease, whether welcoming the Israeli soccer team to glorious Ebbets Field in Brooklyn or being welcomed by airport mechanics in their work clothes.

Hi there!

She greets the crowds whom she loves so much

Her body is most beauteous
being for all things amorous
fashioned very curiously
of roses and of ivory

e.e.cummings

Brooklyn VIPs escort a national VIP at Ebbets
Field, once home of the great Dodgers

Go!

Marilyn kicks off the soccer season for the visiting
Israeli team

Guess who's here!

Mechanics, maintenance men, and the Press hear
that Marilyn is in town – spontaneous
combustion!

In an interview with *Life* magazine shortly before her death, she said, 'In the morning the garbage men that go by 57th Street when I come to the door say, "Marilyn, hi! How do you feel this morning?" To me it's an honor, and I love them for it. The working men – I'll go by and they'll whistle. At first they whistle because they think, oh, it's a girl, she's got blonde hair and she's not out of shape, and then they say, "Gosh, it's Marilyn Monroe!" and that has its – you know, those are the times it's nice, people knowing who you are and all that, and feeling that you've meant something to them.'

Once, shortly after she moved to New York, driving her out to Long Island for a weekend with my family, we were spotted in her open convertible and soon cars were passing us with whistles and shouts and words of cheer. 'Hi, Marilyn. Is that you, Marilyn? Hello . . . good luck!' The 'Good Luck' (often repeated) was a gesture of affection, beyond the tit-and-ass syndrome of the American male. They genuinely wanted to wish her well, they *liked* her. I'm not sure they liked me, her chauffeur, but good will toward her was in the air.

My one crowd-facing scene with Marilyn

occurred in a concert hall, or was it a theatre? It was after the event, I recall clearly, that we were separated; and she was carried away (literally) by the surging bodies going for the aisles and exits. She called out to me (I swear she was giggling), 'Meet me outside, Claude!' The crowd, knowing very well who she was, now turned in my direction: Claude? Who is this guy?

Indeed, who? I was a borrowed husband by agreement with my wife, doing escort service for a family friend. Fortunately, I wasn't famous (poets have to die first), but it bewildered the crowd. I did then look a bit like Claude Rains (several inches taller, I insist). Marilyn had squirmed to a side door, I heard her urgent whisper to someone, 'Let me through, please. Get me a cab, would you? Please?' She was out now, into the street, while I struggled to join her before she was whisked away by God knows who, agents of the evil empire, no doubt. While she was in no real danger, a crowd-induced injury, a fall or trampling, was always possible. I was under orders from my wife to bring that sweet lady back safely. Luck was with us. Someone found a cab, Marilyn was pushed inside just as I emerged from the building. She held the door open, I dived like a halfback; she hauled me up onto the seat, both of us winded. The driver maneuvered through the crowd – dear beneficent dangerous crowd – and finally got us to her apartment door on Sutton Place.

Marilyn paid the cabbie and said to him, 'Take this gentleman to Brooklyn, to his door. He's a poet and might get lost.' She turned to me. 'Great evening, Claude. We left them wondering who you are, isn't that fun? Thank you. Love to Hedda and thank her too. I'll call her tomorrow.'

She gave me one of her quick lovely smiles as she backed out of the cab. 'I left the cab fare in your coat pocket. Good night and thanks again.'

The twenty-dollar bill was more than enough. When I offered to return the change later, she asked innocently, 'What change?'

Foreground: Jack Hamilton, Look *magazine editor, accompanied Marilyn on a walk down Fifth Avenue (he lost her in the crowd)*

Over here!
'We love you, Marilyn'

Main street, side street – crowds wherever she went

ON THE TELEPHONE

Listen, are you sitting down? I'm going to marry Arthur Miller. Would you believe it? I can hardly believe it. We talked about it the last few weeks, and then it happened. He asked *me* to marry *him*! I guess you can call it news, do y'think? Wow!

You'd never guess, I got this framed picture in the mail, ready to hang, from Albert Einstein! Signed: 'To my dear Marilyn, love, Albert.' No, I never met the man. It's no secret I adore Einstein. And Abraham Lincoln. And of course Arthur Miller. What a morning!

Eli Wallach sent that picture of Einstein! He signed it too. Wasn't that sweet of him? Well, if you can't have Albert, I'll take the photo. That Eli, I have to watch him . . .

6am in Amagansett and Marilyn is already on the phone . . .

13

LOVE IN THE CITY

It began, as most love stories begin, in the entranced light of youthful happiness. Arthur Miller and Marilyn Monroe fell in love. They were young, already famous, with Marilyn ready for the most dramatic step of her career. She had just gone through a painful separation from DiMaggio; now salvation beckoned with Miller.

How to explain this awesome, improbable event? Body meeting Mind? Beauty and the Beast? Cleopatra and Antony? Power attracting power? All sorts of theories emerged. Those who tried, both then and now, to explain it soon realized how futile was their task. Let the experts, Freudians, Jungians, mystics, astrologists, or psychiatrists as well explain smoke. Or music. The dumb-blonde image was dead and gone, for certain.

The outdoor wedding took place on July 1st, 1956 in a rural Connecticut village. It was an orthodox Jewish ceremony with the bride recently converted to Judaism, her own mysterious wish. A lawn party on a glorious summer day, with perhaps twenty-five guests and relatives, very few reporters, and all giddy with anticipation and beverage. The bride was beautiful, the groom handsome and looking quite orderly for a writer. They did all the proper things, they laughed, kissed one another repeatedly and allowed themselves to be kissed, drank champagne (the bride's favorite intake), and answered the ridiculous questions always asked at weddings.

I was supposed to be the best man but was bumped at the last moment by a late-arriving relative. (Marilyn gave me an additional kiss for this snub and whispered, 'Don't worry about it.') Mild chaos hovered over the event, not enough to spoil the sweet sense of happiness-to-come. The ceremony began. Observing the Jewish ritual, Marilyn lifted her veil to sip from a goblet of wine, at the same time (I may be recalling this in the wrong order) breaking the ceremonial glass with her foot. She said 'I do' like in the movies, they exchanged rings; the rest is foggy except the day was glorious and more like music than merely weather. The only sad note was revealed to us later: two reporters from *Paris Match*, speeding to the wedding on a motorcycle, crashed some miles off and one was killed.

At the beginning, then, a tender romance with New York City as their playground. The newlyweds both loved the city, the early months of their marriage were celebrated in their Sutton Place apartment and the adjoining terrain: Central Park, further downtown, even a Brooklyn home visit! They were walkers, and surprised themselves by being good conversationalists; it was an idyllic interlude in what would slowly become the stressful adjustment of two people dancing around the showbiz volcano. Given the life and ambitions of the principals, it was hard not to predict trouble. Careers clashing with personal needs: the writer's desire for privacy and silence, the actor needing an audience and adulation.

At this point in his career (1955-56), Miller was under a political cloud. The clown act periodically playing Washington D.C. to alert the populace to the threat of subversion decided he was important enough to attract

Go faster!

Lovers in the left lane

'Never the twain . . .'

. . . but they did

the media, especially with Marilyn in the picture. Communist hunters Senator Joseph McCarthy and Representative Francis Walter sniffed the air. Miller was called to testify before the House committee, joined by Marilyn who appeared with him publicly in defiance of the bad guys (she turned everything into a movie). He denied any connection with 'communist' groups, which prompted Rep. Walter to utter some priceless prose: 'I don't see how we can consistently not cite him because he very obviously is in contempt.' Whereupon Miller, the dramatist, outflanked him. In reply to Walter's question, 'What is your objective in going to England?' (Miller had applied earlier for a passport to accompany Marilyn for her projected film with Olivier), Miller tossed his grenade. 'My objective is double,' he replied, 'I wish to attend a production of my play, and to be with the woman who will then be my wife.'

What a curtain line! Even Marilyn was taken by surprise. Walter staggered off to the cloakroom. To lose to a mere writer! For the image of a dangerous activist had suddenly turned into that of a lover, and lovers are of course incapable of political action (Byron excepted). And who ever heard of a romantic communist? It was clearly an error. Congressman Walter, then up for re-election, added a touch of farce to the comedy. He requested to be photographed with Miss Monroe. Request denied.

The play referred to by Miller was *A View From The Bridge*, first produced in New York and later in London. It became a big success

*Marilyn rowing at New York's most romantic
rendezvous, Central Park lake*

The Hollywood ending, foretold

there, and it had a long run.

Soon after the wedding ceremony, which took place in the summer of '56 in a barrage of publicity, Marilyn flew off to England for part-honeymoon and part-work (it turned out to be mostly all work) as she starred with Laurence Olivier in the filming of *The Prince and the Showgirl*. The picture was a success, and vaulted Marilyn to a new level of stardom, linked with the most illustrious classical actor of the time. It was not a happy relationship – the Actor's Studio method was not exactly Olivier's – but it proved that Marilyn, newly launched from the East (non-Hollywood) coast, was developing as a self-confident comedienne, a role she handled with high skill in her later and next to last film, *Some Like It Hot*.

Back to Hollywood and domestic living in the celluloid jungle, with Miller trying to concentrate on his writing; the East-West shuttle, the pressure of careers, hers and his, continuing...

Love eternal was to last a mere five years.

'See you later, Alligator'

14

AN IDYLLIC
INTERLUDE

15

'TOUCH MEMORY'

I never went shopping with Marilyn, but my wife Hedda did on numerous occasions; I was often a beneficiary of her shopping sprees at holidays. I still have one of her last Christmas gifts, a snappy super-tailored button-down shirt, dark brown with a thin black parallel stripe pattern, which I continued to wear after her death. When it became frayed, I hand-washed it, prolonging its life and wear; it's still with me, endlessly repaired. Some call it madness but I call it touch-memory. I still put on that shirt on special occasions.

My wife reported that shopping with Marilyn was an adventure, whether on Fifth Avenue or Southampton (Long Island), where they'd try on dresses with gleeful abandon. Yes (but you must know this already), she often wore no underclothes, and startled the attendants upon disrobing. When they appeared uneasy at putting her tried-on dresses back on the racks, Marilyn simply purchased whatever she had tried on, all the while cheerfully keeping up the conversation.

During Christmas shopping, Marilyn would buy enough for several dozen people, with a lion's share for Arthur M, plus gifts for his teenage children Bobby and Jane. She enjoyed the banter of store salesmen, and when in doubt she'd call Miller, one must presume, for his advice. Presuming, as well, that she was interrupting his work or, as often the case, his nap. He could nap as diligently as any man.

Gift-giving was always a happy event, especially when the Miller kids were present. I recall a Christmas exchange around the

I'll take it!

Shopping with Marilyn was an adventure

dinner table after dessert. One of Marilyn's gifts to her husband was a box of ties: ten or more, striped, solid colours, fancy tailoring, cotton, silk, a feast of ties. He opened the box and said something extremely literary, like, 'Hey, gee, how about that? Thank you dear, they're beautiful.'

I, who never owned more than three or four ties during any ten-year period, examined them with admiration and possibly envy which my playwright host was quick to catch. 'One for each day in the week and two for Saturday and Sunday,' I observed. 'Much too many for one writer.'

Marilyn clapped her hands. 'Would you like a few, Claude?'

Miller raised an eyebrow.

'Well,' I said, 'I could be talked into it.'

Miller's nostrils flared. He didn't like the turn of the plot: 'Stop stealing my ties,' he growled.

My wife joined in. 'Come on, it's his birthday soon.'

'I don't like people giving away my ties,' he pretended to sulk.

Marilyn laughed. 'You can't wear them all, honey. Give him two.'

'Take one,' he said.

'What about each of you giving me one?' I added, making my move.

'You have mine,' said Marilyn.

'OK,' said Miller gallantly, 'And one for me.'

'Let's have more champagne,' said my practical wife, raising her glass.

16

GOYA AND THE BLACK DEMONS

Dreams of Marilyn . . .
Nightmares of darkness,
of the child who feared childhood.
Voices that screamed at her,
hands that tore at her clothes;
men who invaded the dark,
clung to her hopelessness,
she who cried out to the darkness . . .

At an exhibit of Goya etchings at the Metro-
politan Museum of Art in New York, accompanied by her guide Sam, as she walked,
unrecognized, no make-up, stopping, staring
at Goya's black demons and monstrosities,
Marilyn said to him, 'I know this man very
well, we have the same dreams. I had these
dreams since I was a kid.'

Through years of psychiatry, Hollywood
star wars, lovers, break-ups, husbands, divorce – those demons never exorcised. And at
night, the pills . . . and the demons again.

Dark nightmares, and romantic obsession.
From Goya to Rodin. Years later, she stood in
that same museum, with a different guide
(myself), staring at Rodin's vision in white
marble, 'The Hand of God'. She was the
young sensual woman in the embrace of a
man, both in the sheltering hand of God. This
was a different dream, the very opposite of the
other, of love and happiness and culmination,
a dream denied her. She stood before this
vision, transfixed, finger at her lips.

Dark nightmares and romantic obsession

AUTHOR CONFERENCE

Certain commentators, women especially, say that Marilyn was a 'victim' of the Hollywood system. How do you feel about that, Sam?

I don't agree.

Neither do I, it's too easy.

You can say that she was crushed by forces beyond her control, personal weaknesses, drugs and pills. That isn't the same as being a victim. At the beginning, maybe you could use that word, low pay, all kinds of hours, industry exploitation . . .

I think women want to use her as a symbol, to evoke sympathy through her struggle and, rightly so, given the cultural and economic factors, to see it as a political thing.

But you know, Norman – we've both lived through it – that Marilyn fought back, something your ordinary victim doesn't do. She fought the studio and its contract tyranny, she fought for and won small but important victories, such as script approval, choice of director, other controls . . . you can't call her a victim, period. It isn't simple with Marilyn. Nothing is.

17

MARILYN LOVES HUGO AND VICE VERSA

It may have seemed like Beauty and the Beast to some, but Marilyn and Hugo loved one another deeply. She worried about her basset hound, especially about his depressions. Her doctor told her that animals can sometimes be cheered up by a small shot of whiskey.

Did Handsome Hugo like the hard stuff? He never said, but he's been seen (I have seen him) on more than one occasion to swallow a teaspoon of eighty-six proof tenderly administered by Marilyn. He would then stand still, turn, stare, sneeze, and do a kind of wobbly dance, possibly even offer a smile, which bassets rarely do. Whatever it was, he swallowed, and the days of his dogdom were lightened.

Marilyn's worries may have been induced by Hugo's peculiar doggie hazards, such as, for instance, how to put it . . . the basset, as you may know, is a low-slung animal, moving close to the ground. Marilyn was anxious (she confided to me) that in hurrying over the rocky country terrain of their farm, Hugo's low penis might possibly strike a stone. She'd cry out merrily, 'Be careful, Hugo!'

18

'A TREE AND GRASS PERSON'

19

PLAYMATES
FOR A DAY

A motherless child, Marilyn loved children. Her lifelong, unsuccessful attempts to bear a child proved to be her greatest regret. We know she had numerous miscarriages, an ectopic pregnancy, and abortions. The path to motherhood was not to have a happy ending. But she loved children; the playful spirit of the child lurked in her eyes, her walk, her psyche, particularly her laugh. That inner child stayed with her to the end.

Sam taught her a few things about the camera and she surprised everyone by taking some fancy shots of my family. For some reason she liked jumping shots, I guess she liked the exuberance and playfulness of the body in motion.

Three Gemini children fated to meet and play: Marilyn and Edie, born June 1st; and Patricia close behind, May 30th. Edie and Patricia, children of Marilyn's friends, barely teenage, and Marilyn in her mid-twenties, and ageless.

June 1st. Birthday for two! As Sam, father of Edie, recalls that day: 'Marilyn was so excited. She called – she was staying at the St Regis here in New York – and said, "I've got two tickets to the Ringling Circus, Joe D left them for me. I'll take Edie." And off they went. Marilyn wore a skirt, a loose blouse, no make-up, a wig wrapped in a babushka like a scarf around her head. Edie I remember with lace-trimmed bobby sox, her hair tied in a bun and white dainty gloves. Both girls, a big sister and a kid sister, left the hotel lobby. Outside on the sidewalk was a mob of Marilyn's fans. She went through the crowd, unnoticed. She

got as far as the corner of Fifth Avenue, stopped, turned around and went back to her suite in the Hotel. When she emerged, there she was, no wig, no babushka, make-up, she looked like herself – Marilyn. She was mobbed and happily signed every last autograph.'

We switch to the circus itself, the Ringling hoopla and hubbub, and Edie's memories: 'Marilyn and I had two center seats up front. We were munching away at popcorn and cotton candy. Emmet Kelly the famous clown was doing his broomstick routine. He suddenly noticed this beautiful blonde, not me, chewing at the candy. He swept his light to her section and completed his act. It was like I remember once with Daddy in Madrid at a bullfight when the bullfighter tossed the bull's ears and his funny Mickey Mouse hat to a beautiful lady in the stands. A little later a group of circus hands came down the aisle to Marilyn's seat. Their spokesman said, "Excuse me, miss, but aren't you Marilyn Monroe?" She smiled at them and said, "No, I wish I was, she's so beautiful." The spokesman said, "We have a bet, three of us said you were and the other three said you weren't." She replied, "I'm sorry if you lost, but thank you for thinking I'm pretty like Marilyn."'

Another day, date uncertain but in that same period; the other child, my daughter Patricia, tells of her playtime with Marilyn. 'Once when my parents were visiting her, I became bored with the adult conversation and found myself wandering through the other empty rooms. As I passed Marilyn's bedroom, a large box on a table by the window caught

I'll be your friend

'Edie, if you want to call me, just call out "Hey
you or hey there or haystack"'

my eye. It looked like a huge metal tackle box. In a moment of curiosity (and bad manners) I lifted the lid and peered inside. It was filled with cosmetics of every description: lipstick, eyeliners, mascara, brushes, sticks of what must have been stage make-up. I was fascinated by the array of hundreds of little jars, bottles and compacts. So engrossed was I in exploring this unusual and interesting find that I didn't hear the sound of footsteps coming down the carpeted hallway. Marilyn discovered me nose-deep in her make-up box. She acted like it was the most natural thing in the world to find me there and before I could even feel embarrassed, she had plunked me down at her vanity mirror and said that since I

was so intrigued by the art of make-up she would show me how to do the job right. The next twenty minutes or so I was in a kind of dream as I watched her skillful hands transform my unremarkable kid's face into something that even I might have called glamorous. My eyelids glimmered, my cheekbones were highlighted, my mouth was rosy with color – why (I thought exultantly), I could pass for seventeen! Not content with doing a partial make-over on this willing pupil, she also did my hair (which usually fell every which way around my shoulders) up in an elegant French twist. Then, oh so proud of her handiwork, she happily took me by the hand back to the living room to show me off to the grown-ups.'

Good company

Photos taken by Marilyn of Norman, Hedda and
Patricia Rosten

20

AMERICAN BUCCOLIC

A summer idyll, a new marriage . . .
Beach at Amagansett, far from cities,
where lovers have water and sun and one
another.
Marilyn as a beach person, a tree and grass
person,
a playful Aphrodite out of the sea . . .
Here in a hideaway with little space to hide,
stardom pressing in, photographers,
curious watchers, even a helicopter visitor!
But the beaches were nearby, time to escape,
to play and love and plan; on the horizon
the smallest dark clouds . . . years distant . . .

Sam, with his timeless camera, observes Marilyn in the moment of her time: 'I think my camera has caught Hogarth's Shrimp Girl, Franz Hals' sensuous tavern beauty, moments of a sad reflective Saskia, a Hollywood starlet, and a lovely new wife at 6 o'clock in the morning on the telephone in Amagansett, Long Island.'

The summer of 1956 and into 1957, with the Millers in a quiet roomy cottage for days, weekends, or seasons, at the edge of fashionable East Hampton where city folk come to vacation or to show off their clothes and cars. Artists, writers, fishermen, imported and native. Horse shows and trails, and horses roaming outside the Miller cottage (they didn't own one, or ride). Few celebrities (was that a glimpse of Richard Burton and Elizabeth Taylor I caught one day while driving by?), and even fewer neighbors. Willem de Kooning was one; his portrait of Marilyn in the

Museum of Modern Art offended Miller: he hated it, Marilyn was silent. The sculptor Constantine Nivola and his family lived nearby, less celebrities than friends. It was, however, a lonely period. Marilyn was between films (*The Prince and the Showgirl* and *Some Like It Hot*) and perhaps in hiding since she was voluptuously overweight. She lolled in the sun or romped, and would often bike down the road to a small locality a mile or so away called Springs where we lived during those summers. Marilyn would rest and chat and have tea, take walks with Hedda, or sometimes play with Patricia.

We had many happy visits. I'd catch her brooding at certain moments, but these would pass quickly. Miller would join us once in a while, or we'd all occasionally meet for a swim in the Atlantic not too distant. American bucolic, but hardly rural.

21

FEELING
OVER
INTELLIGENCE

In the summer of 1957 she suffered through a pregnancy and miscarriage, a sad repeat for Marilyn. The following year, in Hollywood, she bounced back in the new, confident, brilliant style of *Some Like It Hot*. But the black demons of Goya were returning to her dreams. Work schedules, business pressures, the recurring dependence on sleeping pills, pickup pills, hints in the press of marital problems, innuendos – it was the place she knew so well, too well: the wheeling and dealing movieland jungle.

Marilyn was born in the Industry. She rose from cheesecake stills and bit parts, from starlet to feature player to star. Miller too was a star. During their one collaboration – Marilyn's last film, *The Misfits* – their marriage faltered. It broke apart on the arid sand of the Nevada desert. Each tried to do their best, but the production (business) factors seeped into their personal lives and pulled them down. It is ironic that these two people, who began as idealists, should have taken on the trappings and corruption of the Industry.

All good actors fight for the characters they are playing. In *The Misfits* Marilyn is fighting for the woman that is her. When she cries out near the end of the film, 'You are the killers,' she is talking not only to the men who corner and kill the wild horses, but to all the men who had used and demeaned her. It was a triumph of feeling over intelligence, her own character now fused with the character she was playing. Miller's was the triumph of intelligence over feeling. It may turn out that Miller was less the artist than she.

Her last film revealed a new and deeper side to her talent, perhaps the farthest she would have gone had she lived. There are many who would contend that at the time of her death she had achieved a considerable accomplishment, indeed a fulfilment.

22

TWILIGHT

The last day, August 4th, 1962, in the thirty-sixth year of her life. The hours counting down, the day moving toward darkness. Is there a summation possible? The Goddess, the Golden Girl, Aphrodite, America's darling (for a while), had come to the end of the line. Her career in shambles, her personal life going nowhere, back in the town of her past glory. One might say she had come home to die.

Her two previous loves, DiMaggio and Miller, were continuing on with their lives. Miller had remarried, his new wife bore him a child, reminder of her own failure. DiMaggio would leave the baseball world for the business world. Marilyn had no place to go; in the middle of a new film, she was fired. Booze and pills had now become part of her existence. She drifted among uncertain friends and old lovers in a kind of twilight zone. Then that fatal day of deep depression when her psychiatrist was not available. Her final Father had somehow betrayed her; her real father turned his back long ago; Clark Gable, the kind substitute of her last completed film, had died. She was beyond the power to be saved. Friends, lovers, teachers, a half-sister somewhere, and my wife and I, too, once a port in a storm, now 3000 miles distant. Our dear friend was alone in a room of an incompletely furnished house, the indifferent city around her, and only the telephone close by, solace of the forgotten.

It was a late Friday afternoon of that year when our phone rang in New York. It was her. My wife and I have tried often to analyze that last call. Death was farthest from our minds.

And her voice instantly reassured us: it was high, bubbly, happy, not at all like one preparing to take her life before the next day dawned or trusting in a temporary oblivion of drugs that tragically misfired into death.

Theories would later take hold on the public imagination, for journalism thrives on gossip, conjecture, amateur sleuthing, and wild surmise. And, above all, on sensationalism. Murder. Poison. CIA. Kennedys. Mafia. Stomach pumping. Body snatching and return. As ingenious and attractive as these hints and the clever pursuit of circumstantial evidence are (we were, after all, in Hollywood), there is no hard evidence of murder. Hints, hearsay, some conflicting or suspiciously overlapping details, but most who were around then, witnesses or recallers, are now dead, senile, bored, and the pursuit of 'justice' in this case is will-o'-the-wisp. Let those who wish to cling to murder for the benefit of sales, whose minds run to violence and the exotic, sum it up that way. Questions may always remain. Suicide, even in the case of one who has attempted it many times before succeeding, is too unsatisfying for the public mind; it throws up a finality whereas most Americans like to tease such events to some protracted form, a continuing TV mini-series or soap opera.

As I see it, Marilyn took an (accidental?) overdose; it fitted her character, given the forces crowding in upon her. She hungered for death; let us give her that victory.

As for our phone conversation – among the few calls she made on that final day – one

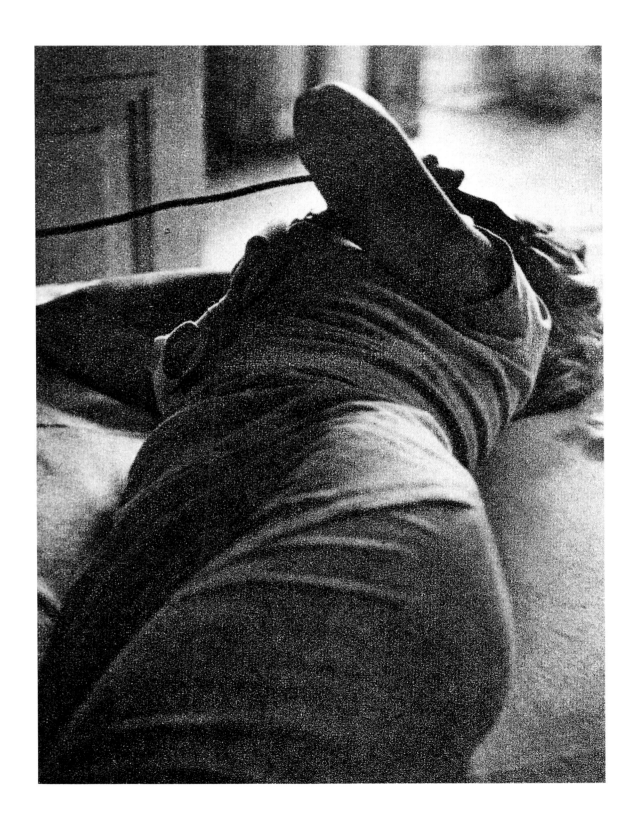

would have to have been prescient or trained in these crises to fully grasp the contradictions. She spoke to both of us, an hour of talk, we passed the phone from one to the other. On the surface it was a happy exchange of news and hopes for the future: she was in great shape (not true); she was planning to begin a film in the fall (fantasy); her house was almost furnished (never to be); she planned to come to see us and then take a gala trip to Washington for the opening of Irving Berlin's new musical, *Mr President*; she was getting film offers from all over the world (doubtful). She spoke excitedly about the new kitchen, the Mexican tiles, the pots, the pans, the stove. She raced on, breathless, gossipy, a little high. Silence, then she repeated How were we? How was I? And over and over, How was Patricia? How she missed us! We were struck by her intensity, as if for a moment she saw us again really as people and friends. Then a rush of new thoughts: it was time to put the past behind and begin to live, let's all start to live before we get too old; why don't I fly out for a visit and talk about the old days of Brooklyn; or, more urgently, she wondered if Hedda couldn't come out even for a weekend . . . What neither of us, neither my wife nor I, could catch was the subtext of that call. A message we missed. Something urgent underneath, her feverish moving from subject to subject. Only the next morning, hearing the sad news on the radio, did we realize what the message was. It was one word: Help.

I had prophesied it years earlier in the ending of a poem I had written to her but never showed her:

You're not to be rescued wholly in this world.
It must be so. As many who are saved,
That many drown. I see you clinging
To rooms, to phones, forgotten to be loved.

She had once written a fragment entitled 'To The Weeping Willow', with these lines:

I stood beneath your limbs
and you flowered and finally clung to me
and when the wind struck with . . . the earth
and sand – you clung to me

She often tried her hand at poetry. It was her way of saying difficult things to herself. If we read limbs as 'branches', she had her wish in death: she became one with nature.

EPILOGUE: A BACKWARD LOOK

Marilyn often referred to me as her 'closest friend'. I'm not sure what 'closest' means. I was not her lover. I thought of myself and my wife Hedda as a single supportive force toward a sweet but troubled human being. My wife believed I loved Marilyn; but so did she. If love is that force, or presence, we both did. We were at peace with that idea. Possibly it was the love of a parent for a child, an older daughter, or a family member whose life was on the wrong track.

In those years, people, friends, were closer. There was more meaning to friend-ship. Today, the pursuit of happiness is more brutally the pursuit of power, its seekers trusting in things rather than feelings. People like Marilyn never quite made it from power to happiness. She had the instinct and reflexes of the poet, but lacked the control.

She was a beautiful, almost other-worldly creature who left behind some of that beauty. And I, the last of that trio, thank her for a brief visitation into our lives.